KU-495-874

Jackass wid him long tail, _____ Bag a co - co com -in down. _____

3 I'm not strong, Sir (3-part round)

The Jolly Herring 62 (in B♭)

I'm not strong, Sir, sure 'tis wrong, Sir, such high notes my voice do strain.

I can't sing a note, Sir, something hurts my throat, Sir, though I try my best 'tis all in vain.

I'm quite hoarse, Sir, so of course, Sir, I cannot sing this round a - gain.

4 Waltzing Matilda

words: A. B. Paterson
music: Marie Cowan
Ta-ra-ra boom-de-ay 53

Once a jol - ly swag - man camped by a bil - la - bong, un - der the shade of a

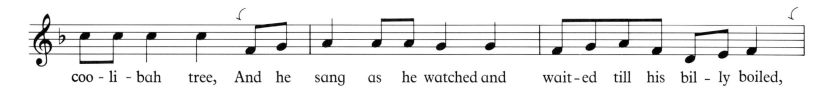

coo - li - bah tree, And he sang as he watched and wait - ed till his bil - ly boiled,

"You'll come a-waltz - ing Ma - til - da with me! Waltzing Ma-til - da, waltz - ing Ma-til - da,

you'll come a - waltz - ing Ma - til - da with me," And he sang as he watched and

wait - ed till his bil - ly boiled, "You'll come a - waltz - ing Ma - til - da with me."

7600 - art, music

high F

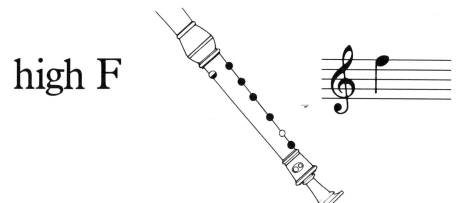

1 Yesterday

John Lennon/Paul McCartney
Ta-ra-ra boom-de-ay 52 (in D)

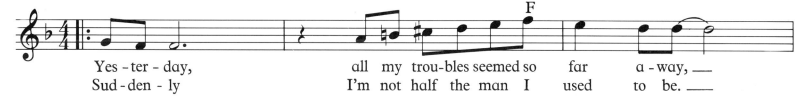

Yes - ter - day,   all my trou-bles seemed so   far   a - way, ___
Sud - den - ly   I'm not half the man I   used   to be. ___

Fine

now it looks as though they're here to stay,   oh   I   be - lieve in   yes - ter - day.
There's a   shadow hanging   o - ver me,   oh   yes - ter - day came   sud - den - ly.

Why   she   had   to   go   I don't know, she would-n't   say.

D.C. al Fine

I   said   some - thing wrong, now I   long   for yes - ter - day. ___

991938885 8

2 Jackass wid him long tail

traditional Jamaican
Mango Spice 20

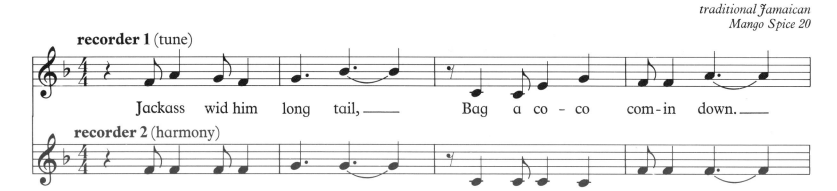

recorder 1 (tune)
recorder 2 (harmony)

Jackass wid him long tail, —— Bag a co - co com - in down. ——

Jackass wid him long tail, —— Bag a co - co com - in down. No

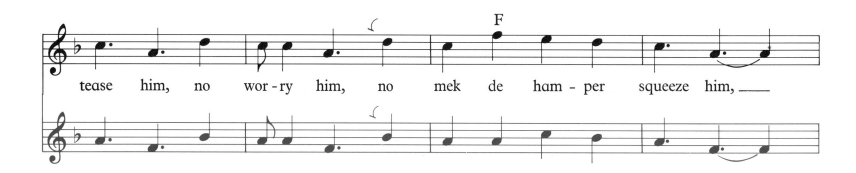

tease him, no wor - ry him, no mek de ham - per squeeze him, ——

5 Silent night

words: Joseph Mohr
music: Franz Grüber

6 Nancy's fancy

traditional

tuned percussion 3 (C, E, F)

right hand

left hand

D.C. al Fine

7 Dorianism

traditional German, arr. Carl Orff
from Orff-Schulwerk: Music for Children, book IV

8 Once I had a sweetheart

traditional
The Jolly Herring 59 (in B♭)

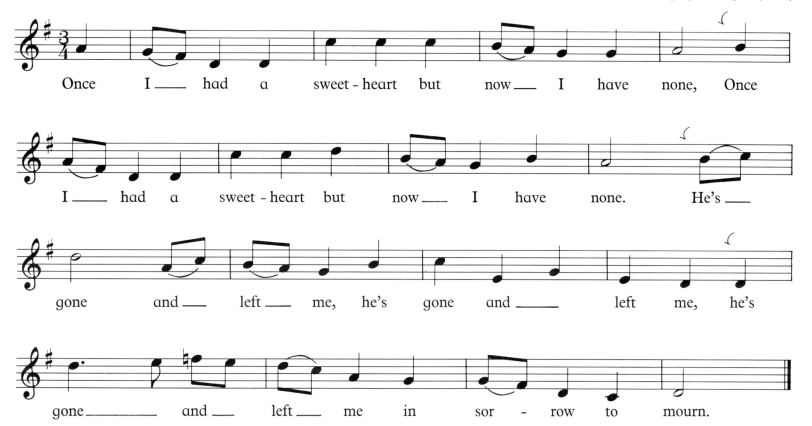

Once I had a sweet-heart but now I have none, Once

I had a sweet-heart but now I have none. He's

gone and left me, he's gone and left me, he's

gone and left me in sor - row to mourn.

9 You are my sunshine

Jimmy Davis/Carl Mitchell
Ta-ra-ra boom-de-ay 16

You are my sun - shine, _____ my on - ly sun - shine, _____ you make me

chords: F

hap - py _____ when skies are grey. _____ You'll ne - ver know, dear, _____ how much I

Bb   C   F   Bb   C

love you. _____ Please don't take my sun - shine a - way. _____

F   Bb   F   C   F

Guitarists: Use a major chord open tuning, then play barre or bottleneck.
Alternatively play conventional E major chords (E, A, B7) with a capo on the first fret.

10 Ta-ra-ra boom-de-ay

Henry Sayers
Ta-ra-ra boom-de-ay

E and F are only a semitone apart, so E♯ is the same as F.

11 Those were the days

Gene Raskin
Ta-ra-ra boom-de-ay 51

guitar chords

Am ... A7

Once u-pon a time there was a ta-vern, ____ where we used to raise a glass or

Dm ... Am

two. Re-mem-ber how we laughed a-way the hours, _____ and

B7 ... E7 ... tacet

dreamed of all the great things we would do. Those were the

Am ... Dm ... G

days, my friend, we thought they'd ne-ver end, ___ we'd sing and dance for e-ver and a

tuned percussion (C, D, E, G, A, B)

cymbal ... *etc.*

bass drum ... *etc.*

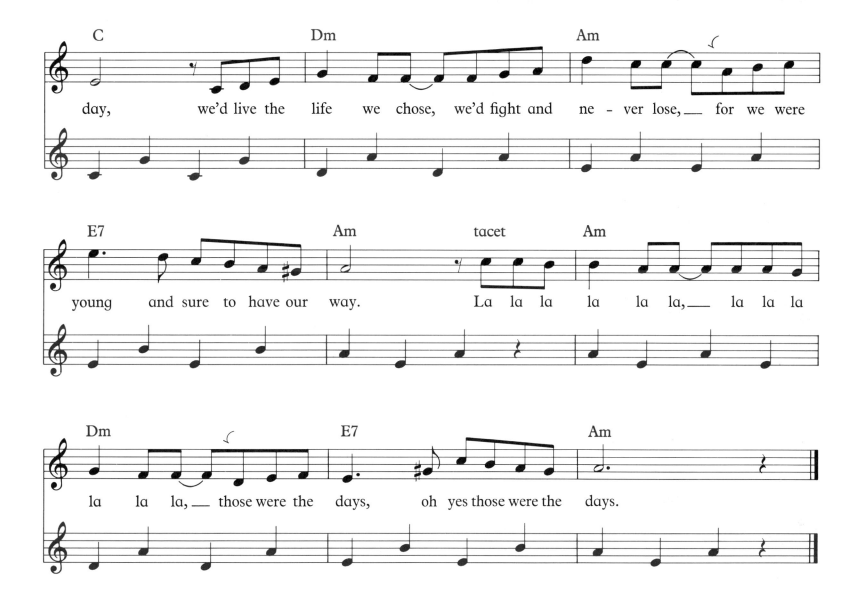

12 March of the kings

words: tr. Coleman/Jorgensen
music: traditional French
Merrily to Bethlehem 21

Three great kings ___ I met at ear - ly morn, ___ with

tuned percussion

cymbals (clashed)

(Three great kings)

all their re - ti - nue were slow - ly march - ing. Three great kings ___ I

met at ear - ly morn, ___ were on their way to meet the new - ly

13 When I'm sixty-four

Percussion

Two untuned wooden percussion instruments, e.g. woodblocks, Chinese blocks,
 claves, or an improvised substitute.

Tuned percussion:

Piano

Bass drum

John Lennon/Paul McCartney
Ta-ra-ra boom-de-ay 11

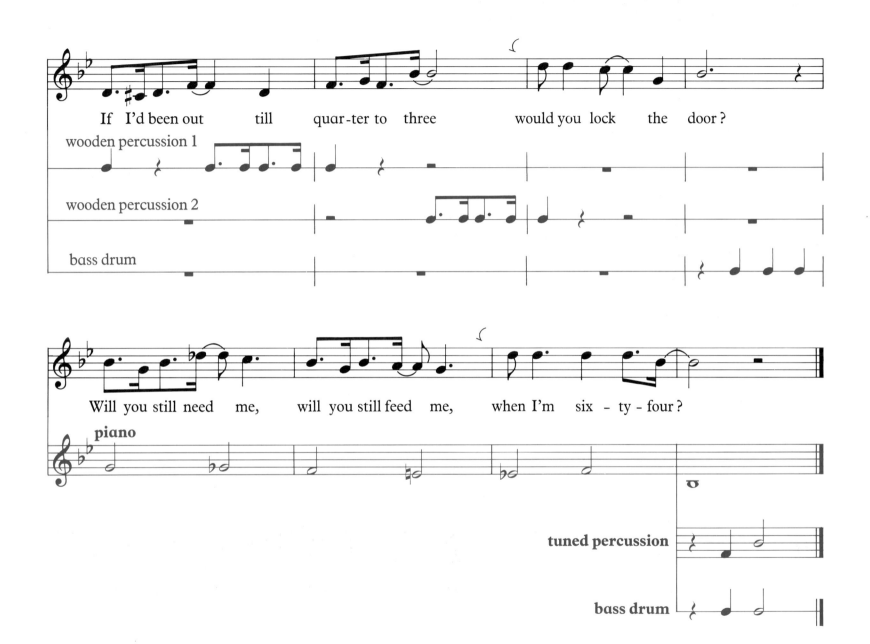

If I'd been out till quar-ter to three would you lock the door?

wooden percussion 1

wooden percussion 2

bass drum

Will you still need me, will you still feed me, when I'm six - ty - four?

piano

tuned percussion

bass drum

high F#

14 Sailing

Gavin Sutherland
The Jolly Herring 70 (in E)

F#

I am sail - ing, I am sail - ing, home a - gain, _____ 'cross the

tuned percussion

guitar chords: A   F#m   D

bass line (e.g. bass tuned percussion, piano, bass guitar)

sea,   I am sail - ing   stormy wa - ters   to be near you,   to be free.

A   Bm   F#m   Bm   A

high G

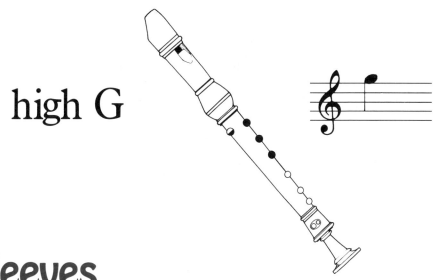

15 Greensleeves

traditional

16 The Wombling song

Mike Batt
Apusskidu 27

Un - der-ground, o - ver-ground, Wom - bl - ing free, the

Wom-bles of Wim - ble-don Com - mon are we, — Mak - ing good use of the

things that we find, — things that the ev - 'ry-day folks —— leave be - hind,

Un - cle Bul - ga - ri - a, he can re - mem - ber the days when he was-

(cymbal and side drum continue as before)

17 Ring of bright water

Betty Botley/Frank Cordell

Where sun and wind play on a ring of bright wa - ter,

that's where my heart - land will be. _____ The deer on the hill in the

first snow of win - ter, the gull in the sky wing-ing free. _____

Percussion: soft wave-like rolls on a suspended cymbal.

18 Sly Mongoose

traditional Jamaican
Mango Spice 19 (in C)

Sly Mon - goose, your name gone a - broad,

Mon-goose slip in - to Bed - ward kitchen, steal out one of his righteous chicken,

Put it in - to his waist-coat pocket, Sly Mon - goose.

19 Country gardens

Morris dance tune

descant recorder 2

high A

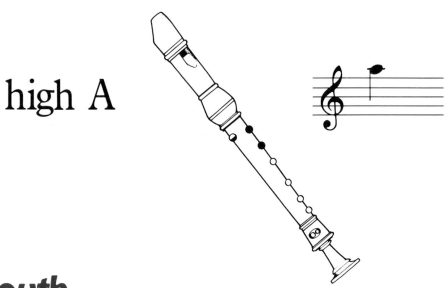

20 Portsmouth

Guitar chords are given in the key of E. Place the capo
on the first fret, and chords fingered for E major will actually
sound a semitone higher, in F major.

E♭

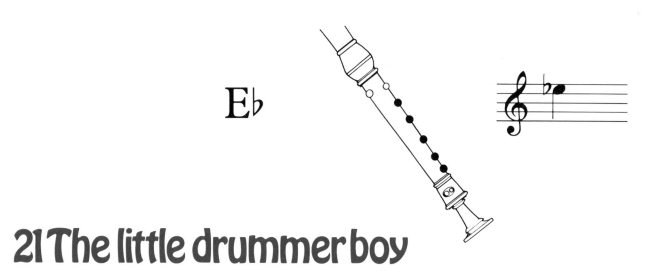

21 The little drummer boy

words: Katherine Davies
music: Czech
Carol gaily carol 11

recorder 1 (tune) – tails up

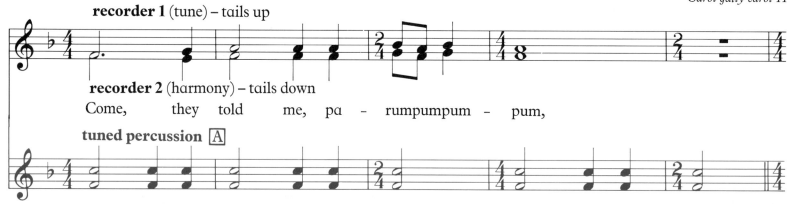

recorder 2 (harmony) – tails down

Come,   they   told   me,   pa – rumpumpum – pum,

tuned percussion A

a   new-born   king   to   see,   pa – rumpumpum – pum,

tuned percussion B

Use low-register tuned percussion if possible.

22 The lightning tree

Stephen Francis
The Jolly Herring 73 (in Bm)

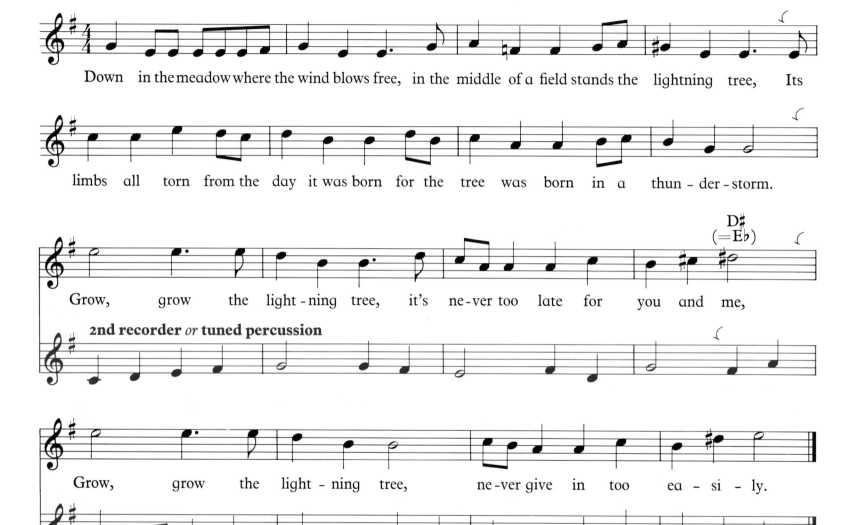

Down in the meadow where the wind blows free, in the middle of a field stands the lightning tree, Its

limbs all torn from the day it was born for the tree was born in a thun-der-storm.

Grow, grow the light-ning tree, it's ne-ver too late for you and me,

2nd recorder *or* **tuned percussion**

Grow, grow the light-ning tree, ne-ver give in too ea-si-ly.

Two syllables appear below some notes. This is because only the first verse is printed here, and it has more syllables than the other verses. Also, a vocal part played on recorder may sound better without too many repeated notes.

low E♭ (or D♯)

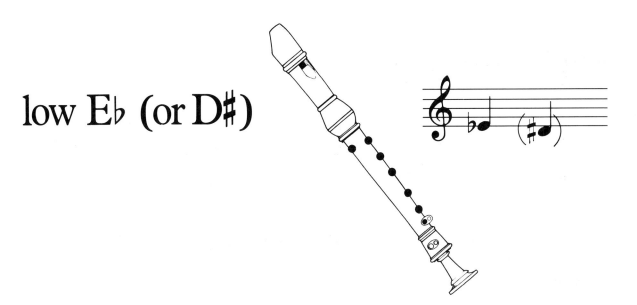

23 The Entertainer

Scott Joplin

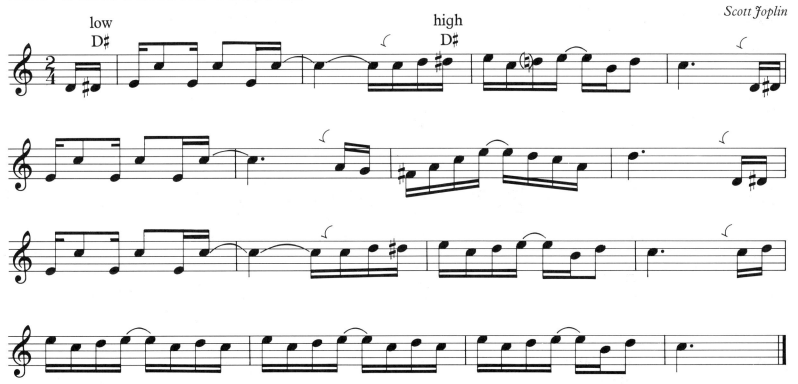

24 A new dawn

Graham Westcott

Acknowledgements

We are most grateful to all the teachers and advisers who have helped us to prepare this book. Our particular thanks to Leonora Davies, Catherine Johnson, Martin Sheldon and Cynthia Watson.

The following copyright owners have kindly granted their permission for the reprinting of words and music:

Chevron Music Publishing Ltd for 22 'The lightning tree'.

EMI Copyright Holdings Ltd for 16 'The Wombling song' © 1974 EMI Copyright Holdings Ltd, London WC2H 0EA.

Island Music Ltd for 14 'Sailing' by Gavin Sutherland, © 1972 by Island Music Ltd.

MCA Music Ltd for 17 'Ring of bright water' © MCA Music Ltd.

Northern Songs for 1 'Yesterday' by John Lennon and Paul McCartney © 1965 by Northern Songs and 13 'When I'm sixty-four' by John Lennon and Paul McCartney © 1967 by Northern Songs. Used by permission of Music Sales Ltd, 8–9 Frith Street, London W1V 5TZ.

Peermusic (UK) Ltd, 8–14 Verulam Street, London WC1X 8LZ and Allans Music Pty Ltd for 9 'You are my sunshine' © Peer International Corp, USA.

G. Schirmer Inc for the words of 12 'March of the Kings' ©.

Schott & Co Ltd for 7, Piece no. 3 in two parts from page 46 of Music for Children book 4 Ed. 4868 (Orff-Schulwerk).

TRO Essex Music Ltd, Essex Music of Australia Pty Ltd and The Richmond Organization for 11 'Those were the days'. © 1968 Essex Music Inc NY assigned to TRO Essex Music Ltd London SW10 0SZ. Reproduced by permission.

Warner Chappell Ltd and International Music Publications Ltd for 21 'The little drummer boy', © 1958 Mills Music Inc/ Delaware Music Corp.

Graham Westcott for 24 'A new dawn' © Graham Westcott.

Every effort has been made to trace and acknowledge copyright owners. If any right has been omitted, the publishers offer their apologies and will rectify this in subsequent editions following notification.

First published 1982 by A & C Black (Publishers) Ltd, 35 Bedford Row, London WC1R 4JH
© 1982 A & C Black (Publishers) Ltd
Reprinted 1982 (twice), 1985, 1987, 1991, 1993, 1996

All rights reserved. No part of this publication may be reproduced, or used in any form or by any means – photographic, electronic or mechanical, including photocopying, recording, taping or information storage and retrieval systems – without permission of the publishers.

ISBN: 0 7136 2166 4

Printed by Caligraving Ltd, Thetford, Norfolk